Wm. Heyen / 2008

Gilgamesh at the Bellagio

KARL ELDER
Gilgamesh at the Bellagio

The National Poetry Review Press
Aptos, California

The National Poetry Review Press
(an imprint of DHP)
Post Office Box 2080, Aptos, California 95001-2080

Copyright © 2007 Karl Elder
All rights reserved

Printed in the United States of America
Published in 2007 by The National Poetry Review Press
ISBN 978-0-9777182-6-9

Acknowledgment is made to the editors of the following publications in which these poems, sometimes in slightly different versions, first appeared.

Beloit Poetry Journal: from *Mead*: "Agnostic Radio," "Anna Banana," "The Chills," "Everything I Needed to Know," "The Haves and Have Nots," "A Mystery," "Original Sin," and "The Resignation"; from *Z Ain't Just for Zabecedarium*: "American Bovary (The Cosmetician)," "A Disappearing Act," "Love in the Time of Quantum Mechanics," "Making History," "The Rookery," "Shining," "Urban Dénouement," and "The Watchers and the Watched"

Black Warrior Review: "Gilgamesh at the Bellagio"

Free Verse : "Transportation," (awarded first place in a contest sponsored and judged by Marilyn Taylor)

The National Poetry Review: "Acme Academy of the University of Megalomania at Melancholy," "Arse Poetica," and "Pastoral Ethereal"

The Newport Review: "Sleepover"

qarrtsiluni: "Professor Lucifer in the Arena of Angels" and "Snapshots"

River City: "Tall, Dark, and Handsome"

September 11, 2001: American Writers Respond: "September Ever After"

Spectaculum: "Child Sisyphus," "The Correspondent," "Five July," "The Likeness," "The Matter of the Immaterial," "Two Voids," "The Wild and the Domesticated," and "The Word"

Standing Wave: "Sound"

Typo: "On Revolution"

Update, the Magazine of Lakeland College: "Dialectic"

Mead appeared originally as a chapbook from Marsh River Editions under the title *Mead: Twenty-six Abecedariums*. My thanks to its editor, Linda Aschbrenner.

Herewith the author also expresses his appreciation to the editorial board of *Beloit Poetry Journal* for its unanimous selection of the group of eight poems indicated above from *Z Ain't Just for Zabecedarium* for the 2005 Chad Walsh Award and for its nomination of poems from *Mead* for a Pushcart Prize; to the Council for Wisconsin Writers for the 2005 Lorine Niedecker Award and, in 2006, the Posner Book Award honorable mention for *Mead: Twenty-six Abecedariums*; to the editors of *The Best American Poetry 2005* for reprinting "Everything I Needed to Know"; to the editors of *Poetry Daily* for reprinting the eight poems from *Mead* that appeared in *BPJ*; to the editors of *Verse Daily* for reprinting "A Disappearing Act" and "Making History"; to the Lakeland College Board of Trustees for a sabbatical leave; and to Beth Ann Fennelly for her selection of and gracious introduction to "Gilgamesh at the Bellagio" featured by *Black Warrior Review*.

Cover Art:
Unique Forms of Continuity in Space by Umberto Boccioni

Umberto Boccioni. (Italian, 1882-1916). *Unique Forms of Continuity in Space*. 1913 (cast 1931).
Bronze, 43 7/8 x 34 7/8 x 15 3/4" (111.2 x 88.5 x 40 cm). Acquired through the Lillie P. Bliss Bequest
Museum of Modern Art

Author photo by Glenn Thiesenhusen

Contents

I. Mead

Original Sin	13
Everything I Needed to Know	14
Anna Banana	15
Sleepover	16
Child Sisyphus	17
Sound	18
The Human Condition	19
The Matter of the Immaterial	20
The Wild and the Domesticated	21
Two Voids	22
The Resignation	23
Tall, Dark, and Handsome	24
The Chills	25
Transportation	26
Five July	27
The Correspondent	28
Agnostic Radio	29
On Revolution	30
The Word	31
Dialectic	32
The Likeness	33
September Ever After	34
The Unsung	35
The Haves and Have Nots	36
On Unconditional Love	37
A Mystery	38

II. Gilgamesh at the Bellagio   39

III. Z Ain't Just for Zabecedarium

The Unknown	51
Eden Overgrown	52
The Be and the End-All	53
A Part of Speech Apart	54
Pastoral Ethereal	55
American Bovary (The Cosmetician)	56
Love in the Time of Quantum Mechanics	57
American Masque	58
Making History	59
The Rookery	60
Acme Academy of the University of Megalomania at Melancholy	61
Urban Dénouement	62
Divine Comedies	63
Another Country	64
Professor Lucifer in the Arena of Angels	65
Zucchini Surprise	66
Tabloid Behemoth	67
The Watchers and the Watched	68
Arse Poetica	69
Ode over a Coffee Table Book	70
Less Is More	71
A Routine Physical	72
Snapshots	73
Loss	74
Shining	75
A Disappearing Act	76

To Brenda

I. Mead

❖ Original Sin

"A ain't just for applesauce," the alpha
bet Adam, who bemoaned the fact they were
classmates, of the same school, no less, Adam
dumb as he was, as Alf was smart as. "In
each of my hands," Alf then posed, "I hold peach
fuzz but no peach. Now *what*," he said, "have I
got?" Adam's eyes jerked side to side as if
his head were caught in a vice, the riddle
inside, as if Eve might have the answer,
just over his shoulder, mum. "My word, what
kind of conundrum have these two cooked up?"
lisped Adam as though a condom sheathed his
mother tongue or a code invaded his
nose. "Come home hungry and what do I get—
original thin and a thickening
plot, as though Elmer Fudd's become my lot."
Querulousness being father of prayer,
right away the Good Lord God Almighty
spoke: "Good grief, man, as though that knot in your
throat were not enough, you're clueless too. Your
ewe is lost, your luck is fucked, dah dah dah/
dit dit dit dah / dit / dit dah dit." Adam
wished he'd been born all alone. Now, rated
X, with no recompense, he in his myth
yammers on, stewed with the sour juice of
Zeus—how *he* might have made him president.

❖   *Everything I Needed to Know*

Ashes, Ashes, we fall on our asses
because the teacher has us. Rodeo
clowns make about as much sense, but then they
don't graduate from kindergarten that
early either. Neither could they have had
for their teacher Mrs. Cunningham, whose
grave countenance no kid had the word for:
Her is no bull sitter. Her is squeezing
in chair, knees together. Her is a locked
jaw with lips like a bad ventriloquist's.
Kind of like a lady Clutch Cargo. Or
like the bride of a Nordic Frankenstein,
motherless but blonde, beautiful, and big.
Nobody here knows she has another
occupation but me. I'm her little
Picasso, her baby ham, and cunning.
"Quit staring, Karl Curtis," she says, looking
right at me. She knows I know for a split
second she disappeared and does not want
to reveal her secret identity
underneath. I know she knows I draw some
very naked ideas. Later, when
we go around and tell in tones like the
xylophone's, girls always first, what it is
you want to be when you grow up, I say
Zorro because a poet needs a mask.

❖ Anna Banana

A. B. C. D. E. F. G. H. I. J.
Bird. What's a J-Bird, anyway? How'd it
come to be naked? Maybe it's a she.
Does she live in a tree? A. B. C. D.
E is for Eve, whose apple isn't just
for her, the teacher, especially when
getting her pupil's goat's more savory.
Here's a little ditty: 1. 2. 3. 4.
in a boy child's best prepubescent voice.
Jump rope's like that. They've got you hopping, then
K-I-S-S-I-N-G in a tree.
Lust? Ask around. On any playground *like*
means love. Love is yuck. Strictly for grown-ups.
No respectable kid carves or draws hearts
on oaks or walks if the object's not to
pimp your buddy. As for girls? Few are the
queens keeping to an airy castle while
royalty's right ventricle's still AWOL.
Surely goodness and mercy shall follow
them, female and male, Jill and Jack, up, up,
up the hill and back, back, back until all
virtuosity they once lacked appears
without warning to dance, dance away doom.
X, God knows, is but one sex chromosome.
Y is why it takes two to fandango.
Zoom in. Zoom out. Big and small, they're human.

❖ *Sleepover*

A is for the last letter in *zebra*,
b being third and first in the word *bra*.
See, there is this real old junior high joke.
Dumb as it was, it seemed like silence woke
everybody in the tent up, as if
for the moment even the town sheriff,
gone elsewhere on patrol, had the same dream.
How else to explain a girl's muted scream
in sync with a song on a radio?
JANE-NEXT-DOOR! IN-JOE'S-NEW-CAR-PARKED-WITH-JOE!
Kid clawing kid to get at the tent flap,
lucky that no one got kneed in the lap.
Mostly over, all we could really see
no male has not seen, when, her back turned, she
offered up her hands with a downward look,
paused in that winged-woman's gesture of hook
quizzing eye. What an afterimage turned
rook! What a buzz of hisses, cuss words turned
spit on a canvas gone dark, suddenly,
this nest turned hive of bitter-sweet honey
until the drone of hormones died—the queen,
voluptuous in a shared vision, lean
with lights now flown. Who'd save us but our own
Xavier, a.k.a. Dick or "Bone"
Youngblood, with a line to make the ground quake:
"Zebra? It's the b-biggest one they make."

❖   *Child Sisyphus*

As a kid you'd kick a stone all the way
back home where there was a strew of stones you'd
come to own, it being your habit that
drove them there, their value their uselessness
even to you, who without labor learned
for good the pious worth of no reward.
(Grace may have had something to do with it,
halfwit that you were [and are?], like the star
idiot, your gift unaware you're it,
John Q. Public's joke about the poet.)
Kitty-corner on ungraded road—there
lay great supply, gravel sparkling like new
money piled blindingly high on Old Man
Nohow's drive beneath a cat-like and wide
open eye, that stiletto's slit of a
parted curtain its pupil. The peril?
Quandary, pure and simple, a certain
rush that says you're caught whether you thought to
steal or not, a knowing before knowledge
temptation's always there for the taking.
Urchin turned perfect angel, verve become
verse, now you flounder instead of plunder
with lines recidivous toward the end,
xebec-like in the beginning under
your pirate's patch, your squint, that aim and thrust,
Zarathustra's truth all's written in dust.

❖ Sound

"An almost voice" was how the child described
both the groan of the ice and the quiet
created by it, the latter of which
didn't seem to happen second nor first,
exactly, but overlap as though snow
falling to rise higher had smothered one
ghost in the form of the child's reflection,
having inspired another appearing
in the garb of white noise, a whisper in
January begun as June thunder.
Knee high on both banks, drifts broke into smoke,
lifted large as though the drifts themselves were
more smoke, amorphous walls winding along
narrow and sometimes gnarled space, riverbed
opening and closing. Still, the child would
pay no heed to the scene, nor would the child
quake before the sound, until sight and sound
are one, as when one understands without
sensation that a fissure has occurred,
the first on the surface of a mural
you and I can't see, except to say we
view it vicariously: the black of
white, vista to the hidden visage of
Xanadu whereto the child in us all
yearns, yet stands in a blind tributary
zigzagging to the dark waters of night.

❖ *The Human Condition*

All one can reasonably ask of the
body—whether sane, suicidal, or
crazy—is some serviceability,
donned since birth like an earth suit for the soul,
elastic or calloused as it need be
from soft spot on top of a toddler's head
grown closed to warts like braille removed from soles,
heaven but one hell of a way to go
into the valley of the shadow and
just for never having lived, trying to
keep off the grass, having turned down the glass,
lust more of an aphrodisiac than
mead, sip of nectar neither the spirit
nor lip dare partake for fear of a new
old need to kill like when one slips off the
pedals, dizzy if not drunk with speed, and
queers the genitals, pain so curious,
rather, hurt so furiously numb that
sex becomes a question mark, becomes a
test of one's ability to contin-
ue in the service of any species
vulnerable and thus vexed as our own,
whores we all are to states of happiness,
extras even as we play the role of
young or old in a feature produced by
Zero Mostel and Edward O. Wilson.

❖ The Matter of the Immaterial

Aretê declines our invitation.
Born blind to all but visible light, Earth
can nevertheless sense its presence as
dogs, cats, birds do too—wild or domestic.
Even ants. And elephants—African,
for a fact, or Indian with ears not
gargantuan so much as they're more gray
hide hiding from us in hordes of the dead,
inching toward perfection in tight herds,
jockeying for protection, ears spread, a
kind of wall built in spite of tremors heard
long ago. Aretê is wind coaxing
men same as beasts by blowing at their backs.
Now and then the ease with which they take sail
overwhelms as if air and their flesh are
part of a conspiracy animals—
quislings they are who don't aspire to the
ranks of heaven—without wings are heir to.
So why all the fuss to see around his
transparentness? Is it because of us
you, Aretê, are thought to exist? Or
vice versa? Perhaps you stand outside our
window; perhaps we bore you to be born,
xenogenetic that you and Earth are,
your lives like the black and white halves of the
zebra's hide—stark, whole, and proverbial.

❖ *The Wild and the Domesticated*

"Animals are our window to the soul."
"Beware of bears bearing barracudas."
Cats? That's not cowering in that crouch, while
dog's a different breed of cat, we say,
except when it rains "cats and dogs." When it's
falling cats and dogs, we're talking the grand
"G-whiz," the "By-God-the-end's-near-if-not-
here." Is that just us hosing ourselves, when
in reality it's just as profane,
just as insane, to ask of the mind, that
keeper of the imagination, to
leave the cage door ajar, when it cannot
matter the occupants are elephants
nosing through the bars of a circus car
or pissants? Because outside's a trap. The
poor animal—mammal, insect, or of
quill—whether wed to the weather or a
ripe bed of dung, is part of a larger
scene revolving, so anything strange we
think we see we've seen, is one of a theme
under a cataract called moon. And as
velocity's the trick of film, as a
wave's a blur of clarity, images
xed into one—soul's, too, an illusion.
"You ought to take your popcorn at home," say
Zenists, and they mean it, body and mind.

❖ *Two Voids*

Angel ovaries and aviaries
bear similarity dictionaries
cannot reveal nor conceal. It's a feel
derived from the common potential for
emptiness fanned by wings. Think of the white
figurine sometimes seen in antique shops
got from God-knows-what, Madonna poised to
hear what cupid, straining on his tiptoes,
is about to whisper in her right ear
just as the child tucked under her left arm
kicks, squirms, worming a portal through something
like marble perceived as invisible—
more real than the reality around.
Now *there's* a counterpart for the value
of nothing in particular if that
particular thing's something cutesy sweet
cupid sings. If when, though, all is said, Round
Rascal and Chubby Cherub happen to,
say, bring news—the messiah first and then
the messenger—heaven's certain to be
upstaged, its curtain, like a veil on a
virgin, is bound to spill, turning white gray
with weather, at last matching myths with this
xenolith, air everywhere thick with wings
yet nowhere for a feather to land, a
Z to the power of zillions, falling.

❖   *The Resignation*

Ace-deuce-tray-lady-kink—another hand
busted before it began. If the whore
could have only come up a four, your king
down, dirty as it may be, might have been
enough to best the better, to call his
flush or shush a bluff in this two-fisted
game named stud—misnomer if ever you
heard one. Pud poker would be more like it—
aye, Mate, even Watergate, a ship you'd
jump but didn't dare, your stroke weak as your
kick. The captain—alias luck—has you
lashed to her mast. You're her chump, her Richard
Milhous Nixon, not one known to know a
noose from a knot. Still, once upon a time
once a month while a sailor in the South
Pacific, seemed you sent home every pot—
Quaker or not. It's how you financed the
race, your California congressional
seat. It's how you came to be beat then won
the presidency to lose it again.
Us? We all were winners and losers too—
voters with a voice, finally, as you
waved the sign for peace, arms a V then an
X, that nix, that quick fix, ducking from sight.
You understood the Law of Averages.
Zapruder, after all, might have filmed you.

❖ *Tall, Dark, and Handsome*

A look on three women's faces enough —
by Christ enough — to make ten men jealous;
caught in a wave of quiet wails, the word
dead bobbed to the top, sank, and suddenly
everything there in the checkout line stopped.
For a second I thought the president
got it. Who would have guessed the king instead?
How were subjects in Springfield, MO to know
in the first place he was *ill*? Heavy? Yes.
Just a tad bit overweight. Yet still those
keen tabloid-cover collars, that killer
look I, at nine, commenced to cultivate,
my mother's mirror seemingly etched by
none other than his image, his svelte voice
on in the background and my face in the
proscenium in spite of the flaking
quicksilver, comb in one hand and white and
red crimped tube of Brylcreem in the other.
Sculpture. Pure sculpture. Adonis with duck
tail. And that part I played in the play — no
understudy for a half-tragedy
vied more for the role, his tale with a tail,
with a tailor whom, should the body be
exhumed, we'd call The Cat That Gave the King
(Yancey? *Lansky*) His Cool: white suit, white shirt,
zaffer tie. To die yet glow in the dark.

❖ The Chills

Awe, we know, is opposite of *ennui*,
beauty being the form, the good worm to
churn the soil of even the darkest souls.
"Dig, thus, your own grave to dance upon it,"
every poet I've dug from Poe on down
forewarns. Yet it's not lore for which I bore
goosebumps today, the first time in months, nor
horror before a mirror, but love of
inspiration, insight flying blind like
jagged lightning, mind to mind, across a
kindred sky. Alone on my way home, a
lull in an otherwise dull day at work,
my finger hits the PWR button and,
now, like the air bag went off, something like
ozone fills the van, liquid emotion,
perfection in the raw that saw—you can
quote me—hair stand in my ear to then lean,
reaching for the origin of the storm,
speakers speaking in tongues, licks electric,
tons of nuance and that shrill demand you
understand: "I am what I am, Edward
Van Halen." I thank God for the goddamned
wonder of it, that energy, the gift,
x for all your problems solved if only
your answer were not a mystery, that
zone more like home than the earth where you live.

❖   *Transportation*

A car should take you where you want to go,
boast a bit of personality, but
claim no soul. So why so hollow having
done away with this one, a van, sold—not
expunged like the rest, towed I mean, more beasts
for the bone yard—when a hundred thirteen
grand ought to be enough for anyone.
Here we're talking miles, of course, not moola:
in ten-plus years four trips around the world.
Just think of the tenths. Figure the inches!
Kept I it another minute, why I'm
likely to have done run out of road or,
more likely, luck, luck being a function
no less of grace than of space to live it.
O for another junket in my junk—
PT Cruiser be damned—though I had no
qualms the moment I signed, sacrificed all
rightful claims in exchange for money down.
So I scrawled a second time, transferred the
title to a John Someone whom, you'd think,
you might recall his entire name except,
very sudden, dumb as a manikin
with seizures of sentimentality,
Xmas come and gone, you, I, you, you chump
you, are transported here, an untethered
zeppelin for a sober head now instead.

❖ Five July

Along the curb where asphalt meets concrete,
bridging the crack, a flattened snake of pitch
crawls, an ill-conceived trope stretching up and
down the street in this early morning heat
each inch of which is without shade as we
face a sun that seems but some hundred feet
going nowhere if not here, and I bow
head and cap, apart from the fact ahead
is a find one could call phenomenon
just as easily: dimes, five, brilliant, some
kid must have dropped and then somehow forgot.
Luck and/or lie of the eye, they are what
much of the walk I had sought—the unearned,
no-frill metaphor, an afterimage
of the grand finale the night before,
pummeled as we were by bursts in clusters
quasar-like, more laser-like than white and
round—dimes alive in limelight, Lucifer's
subwoofer for accompaniment, and
the atmosphere pure cosmic theater
under the cover of the colors of
Valhalla without war, celebration
without clouds, heaven without surrender—
Xmas without December. Speechless for
years, I raise a cold glass of water like
zinfandel and toast to old infidels.

❖ The Correspondent

Ah, the entertainment value, Stupid:
Bubba hugging bimbo, though bonobos,
cousins of the chimp, most promiscuous
devils—without demons, even in their
environs, in their glass house with the whole
freaking human zoo right out their window—
get my vote. But I'm just a journalist.
Hubris is my beat. Pennsylvania
is the name of the street. Jaywalk in this
jungle and they pull your credential. Cross
King Kong and your sweet meat is ever so
lovely to excrete. Objectivity?
May whoever in the audience would
never succumb to such illusion come
on down. Savvy that suave is what every
producer can never get enough of,
Quasimodo, bimbo, or bonobo.
Reporters? Well, you've heard of Heisenberg.
Some say we play the chorus in the play.
They say that we—not his thing—foil the king.
Understand it's you who make or break news.
Viewers have to be there for the viewing.
Watch your watch and we kill the funeral.
XYZ (Examine your zipper). If
your zipper is down, no news is good news.
Zipped? You're not with the program. Deadbeat. Whacked.

❖ Agnostic Radio

Agnostic Radio. Maybe there could
be commercials like HBO's got on
CBS, and Christian Radio would
devour late night spots. It could lend the
emergency broadcasting system's trill
fabulous new meaning. Somewhere, with time
gone by, angels might be ripping off their
headsets at the shrill memory of fear
inherent in a mindset that includes
Judgement Day. Instructed to stand by, to
keep their hands off the dial or—in a more
lavish era—the scan button, they knew
mothers would be separated from their
newborns, husbands from wives, that their lives would
officially be over before the
program manager administered pop
quizzes even, let alone returned to
regularly scheduled programming. Sow
seeds of doubt in sentient creatures so
traumatized, and souls will sprout where are holes.
Under like circumstances the human
vole might not be angels' alien, but
with its own blind though visionary and
xenomorphic metaphysics of forms
yet see itself as beings before souls.
Zookeeper beware of tunnels in air.

❖ On Revolution

Answers aren't necessarily answers.
Boys will not necessarily be boys.
Cancer's no panacea for cancers;
Du Bois, though, was no W. D. Boyce.
Every revolution must have its own
flag, as it is itself a flag, the wind
granting glory to oak and leaf alike.
How quick, however, hubris turns humus
in the long run, which, all said and done, is
justice, if not nature clearing its path.
Kill and be killed or love a little while.
Like it or not, life, love, and luck all leave
much too much to be desired and thus
never nearly enough mulch for the roots
of whatever future there's to be felled,
past or present. As for the last word, its
cue comes not in the sound of a whimper,
rarely a bang, and mostly a whisper.
Sisters are especially apt as was
Thoreau's when at his deathbed she asked, "Do
you want to make your peace with God now?" A
vexing thought for a rebel turned angel.
What could he say but, "I have no quarrel"?
Xanthus, of course, is the name of the horse
young men ride into heaven, bridled, mute.
Zephyr, stud that he was, would have approved.

❖ The Word

Aurora australis or aurora
borealis. Typhoon or a hurri-
cane—the like-same phenomena under
different names, the metaphysics of how
east meets west while south distances itself
from north for purposes of turbulence,
God's great reminder He's there though not here,
hallowed be thy hollow howl, awful as
it may seem, ill, straight from the bowels of hell,
Job's flowing robes whence he stands naked with
knowledge his life's not his own, and just as
locusts play a part in the poem, so
must the human, all the humans, exposed,
naked, though clothed, encapsulated by
O such whirring words mistook for music.
Persons whose more modern costume, whose calm,
quotidian moments are the song's soft
rush of notes, also brace for the crash of
silence, that slow, old crescendo of hope,
taboo and tetragrammaton be damned.
You, the nihilist's ontologist, hear
voices in the formless form of vowels
without consonants, that invisible
excavation of air, that energy
you share, yaw and torque of the primal yawn—
zenith to the teeth, nadir to the tongue.

❖   *Dialectic*

"At what point," mocked Art, "does a falling star
become part of Earth?" Science sensed what the
child had in mind and conjured a response
destined to spawn still another retort:
Every moment is made of more moments;
for us to deny chronology may
gratify the eye yet leaves the viewer
half blind and truth momentarily mute.
"Is it true 'within a circle there are
just as many points as without'? And what
kind of honest number's *that*—'infinite'?"
Life, Art had held, ought to be lived and not
measured by the micron lest it becomes
next its own coffin. So Science taught on.
O what unerring thought he thought he owned.
Perhaps the child would come to see, if not
quickly, that *the brief tails of meteors*
are needles which mend as they rend, that the
sun itself is like the point of a pen
that draws lines of argument full circle,
underwriting thus our universe, the
very author of consciousness—not us,
wholly uncertain, approximate, an
X marking place and time with luck's compass.
Yesterday, after all, is his best guess
zero—ground *and* hour—won't come to pass.

❖   *The Likeness*

A child gazes up at the great man's face.
Bronze becomes them both: The golden bronze of
childhood. The ruddy look of a visage
devoid of flesh, cast with a mournful glance
encompassing all on the hill, he who
for this, a monument to his life, would
gladly take that which only children know,
how to live with wonder when the future
is only as far as a wounded past.
Just as the child seems about to speak or
kiss, maybe, the figure's hand, the child is
led away. There's lots of grass to walk on.
More stones to see. The wind blows its only
note, void of music, of voice, code of and
ode to silence so that people mouthing
perhaps an unknown name off of a stone,
quelled as they are by a child walking by,
recognize in that small, yet open face
something of the form of the monument
that till now hadn't been beautiful nor
ugly, but half-inspired, as if the hands'
vision had been impaired by overly
watchful eyes. Whatever, the likeness wasn't
exactly there. It is here: this child who
yearns in the manner of the now silent
zealot of these people, by them, for them.

❖ *September Ever After*

A transparent tarp you use to haul leaves
belies the eyes, inflates, rises, a great
cape slung by wind over its back, as if
donned by some invisible enemy,
entity without shape. For the form of
fear is never Bear, never Ghost, never
Ghoul. Neither is it evil nor black of
hell. By flames or flashlight the mind still sees
inside the well, while fear's that . . . that thing that
jostles, even should you dwell in certain
knowledge of its presence, your prescience
laughable to the mouth of the hand whose
magic's hardly the glove on your jacket—
nor bite in your billfold—but a cold grip
on your heart. You awaken with a start:
Peace is apple pie without anthrax, the
quintessential mom's art, while you're outside
raking leaves and Dad's about to roll his
sleeves to adjust the carburetor and
timing. And while far more pastoral than
urban, Osama bin Laden's turban's
vacant the picture, which is not to say
war was then more pure, but that rather than
xanthic, leaves, when dervish-like they stood, spun,
yellow-red and blush-gold, in the face of
Zoids *you* stood, pretend sword in hand, deft, bold.

❖   *The Unsung*

Among whole nations at this moment the
brewing of poets! Such assumes that time
contains our beginnings as well as ends,
Dear Universe, that verse be not merely
existential, more angst in a bottle
foaming at the mouth, sunk, on its way down,
ground, eventually, into more sand.
Heaven, on the other hand, is not found
in happy hour nor had for a song. Ask
John Berryman. While you're there, check out the
Kool-Aid stand where—hot damn!—the Jameses are
likely doing booming business, business
meaning not banking with Frank and Jessie
near and Wright and Dickey behind the bar.
O late, great connoisseurs of chaos, must
poetry plunge the best among us in
quixotic behavior while its savior
rests in songs of the unsung? Tomorrow's
seen it all already, it sometimes seems:
the public wants peacocks, wants exotic
uncles, wants suicidal aunts, the new
versions, when the poets only want to
double you over, dance the dance called the
Chiasmus, right your rites without reading
you the riot act or your rights. They want
zeugmas without mead, desire less need.

❖ The Haves and Have Nots

Aye, even Shakespeare would plumb trade for my
bones. At this minute I gots a robin
crowing in clematis crawling up and
down my mailbox planted here at good ole
eleven-seventeen Robin Road you'd
figure patrons might wants to know, 'cause I
gots symmetry and I gots syllables.
Healf? I gots healf in a handbasket 'cause
I gots grandma's shawl 'cause I somehow gots
June pneumonia, gots antibiotics,
killer medicines, pills white as the doc's
light enough to spook hoarse out of horse barn.
Mrs. I gots too—nurse as well as wife.
Now tell me. Is I happy? Is I free?
On count one I gots poetry. On two—
poll the citizenry. Folks here'd sooner
quarantine creator than creation.
Religion? Heaven knows—if it ain't gots
swing, then I ain't gots a godblessed thing
to sing, so you knows I gots religion.
Understand this ain't just ink you read but
veracity come to dwell for all the
while in the sad city Felicity.
Xuthus, great grand chile of Prometheus,
yearns—even Will pines—for what I gots, by
Zeus, be it but birdsong in borrowed light.

❖ On Unconditional Love

A cockcrow might stand for this miracle
but that sun and its cold counterpart moon
concoct a chicken soup illusion that
day may be divided from night just as
egg white's separated from the yolk, when
froth, the stuff of meringue, is far from broth.
Googled (Gospel and hymn), His story is
history, old-world: whether black, white, and
in spite of their pious impunity,
Jesus loves. Suicide bombers. Blown to
kingdom come. Precious in His sight. Red, yell
low, the head the very first thing to go,
minus torso, the limbs akimbo, the
neck weakest link in the human being.
O which came first—innards or injury?
Palestine is real where Israel not
quite quits but—say the hard facts—overlaps
right in Arafat's face. Where, for heaven's
sake, are the maps, the once divine designs,
the city planner's blueprints? Augustine,
you too ought to come clean. You despised you,
vilified your youth, valued the you that
weighed true on redemption's scale, sans God's thumb.
Xes? Not even sex in a mirror.
Yet, chaste, neither is love evil erased.
Zion? What's heaven's hill but hell's shadow?

❖ A Mystery

A pox on talk of the Apocalypse.
Bears we thought haunt the back yard to put a
crook in the shepherd's hook (erected to
dangle seed and peanut butter) aren't the
enemy. Neither is it we. Nor the
foraging bull (moose?), who, like the bears, we
get glimpses of on TV. You'd think our
hour was now, seeing us at the window,
indoors, of course, watching the bird feeder
jiggle to then bob, though these cockcrowing,
kamikaze squirrels aren't the culprits,
leaping, even, off rooftops. So the pole's
mangled though the seed's not scattered. So no
neighbors, though nice and nosy, know of noise—
onomatopoeic onanism—
poised now with their shades raised on all sides to
quash its reoccurrence. As for us, we
rise early as light allows, hoping to
see no garden gargoyle gone nocturnal
turned hell's owl, to kill two birds and test our
unambiguous, unified theory's
veracity: this is the work of no
wind, no wombat. Plotted on a graph the
x-axis's our understanding, flat. The
y? That is the question—despite how few
z's we get—that will never go away.

II. Gilgamesh at the Bellagio

Gilgamesh at the Bellagio

O, it turns out the sonofabitch and
narcissist is immortal after all—
epicure, of late, at faux Lake Como,

The Bellagio, where his spirit reigns,
where fireworks in rain of fountains flower
on the half hour to tunes feigned by the moon;

third he is if body and mind are thirds,
his air of arrogance apparent as
are we, his subjects here in a manner
equal to *air*'s a phononym of *heir*,
equivocal as the hole in our "O"

for what, opposite, looms tall, erect, lit
over the shoulder—no evening, it, in
Uruk or Paris—mock Eiffel Tower,
ready, poised to prick its floating ovum.

Freudian perhaps? Hardly erotic.
Indicative of an imperative
vying for the right of reproduction,
élan if élan's Elvis in the round.

Seen, read assbackwards, the scene is civil.
Indeed, denuded, devils spell evils.
X—*leave it, Enkidu. Dude's an asshole.*

So where to from here for pure, ascendant
entertainment? Helicopter flight to
violate the only virgin in sight?
Exciting as it might seem, why dream when
Neverland is now, our own Grand Canyon?

Enkidu, dude, we'll do the strip, do her
in her innocence, her ambiance of
giant light. Tomorrow. But not tonight.
Hot *damn!* we blink. To think—the only scheme
this bunch had for brunch was a Krispy Kreme,

no protean flash in pan to be gleaned
in neon panoramas paned by foot
(no fleet feat, given how far apart art
eats). Whether, Paul Bunyan, thy bow-legged

thighs were as wide as the St. Louis arch,
even were our Babe the sky, they would, could
not match the stride of Gilgamesh—hollow,

enormous with hunger—thrust and no gait.
Lust like this, we trust, must have purpose, must
enter the arena with more than its
vision to vamp us. *Let's hubba-hubba,*
Enkidu. It's your turn to test your luck,
now, on your own Humbaba. You'll need coin,

time, which there's such scarcity of, and un-

wavering love. Of what? is the question;
err we with answer is to shun the quest.
Love of the test itself? Of itself, love?
Variety's Old Spice, vice? May it be
endgame—no draw, no mate. Should we pocket

the eight by accident or intent, there's
heck to pay—no stroke (backspin, massé or
impeccable English) that circumvents
reticence enough, the cost of gain loss,
those slots sluts that, despite sloth, take their cut,
eschewing the lot of us by at first
enticing us with the thinnest slice of
nonplus pie to reject us like a slug.

Foray for us is we know the plot, can
obviate sure fate, unlike the brides of
Uruk—who knows if they faked it?—lithely
reclining to take it, let alone grooms
that cowered like whipped pups and to whom on
each's tomb, we are left to imagine,
each's widow might have chiseled, "One can
not / omelet con- / coct with chick- / en guano."

F you, too, Gilgamesh, sire of bastards
incarnate, though we are your brothers, blue.
Fuck Humbaba and Bull of Heaven, too.
That's it, Enkidu, yes, that's the spirit—
Eat your own feces, bark at your own moon—
Enkidu, dude, stop. Your point's well taken:

no more dreams for Enkidu. You don't owe

shit when The Shit *owes you. So the mind says.
In the real world, though, body sides with soul,
ex animo. So let us go. Forego
this schism which is, in truth, illusion—
ego, id, superego. Thus it is—
edict: we live. As for identity,
neocortex is more vortex than crown*

such that dull halo and dim bulb aura
ever follow in tow—the id the lead
vehicle flanked by superego and
ego. Semen delivery system?
No, like a metaphysical dildo
that points back to the Bellagio, we
entreat the gods of opulence, of
elegance, fortune, and gastronomy.
Not to preclude circumambulation.

Every rounder knows: you do Vegas, that's
inescapably what you do—you cruise.
Gambling's one ambit; the grandest gambit's
had at the Bellagio, Gil tells us,
that while he prefers goggles, we ought to
employ (nary need to spike our cocktails)
each, our glasses, the waitresses' asses
nicest in town—not an augmented orb,

no, not one, to be found. It's the real deal

in the flesh, those floatation devices
nestled up front, signal in a slit if
ever libido saw it, enough to
turn id into drooling idiot or
eddy of adolescence—the desert's
ebb, *Little* Gilgamesh, as it, throbbing,
now twists in Gilgamesh's fist, an o

the lips on that fish id ogles as chub
woggles under grasp at our gasp, Gil bent
entirely at the waist, wrapped in rapture.
Neither quite autoeroticism,
this, nor, exactly—hand mirror in hand—
your typical gaze into your navel,

the boy, our man Gilgamesh, has a thing
with mother, the *Uber*-mother, whose name,
Eternity, is written here in great
numbers and which, it turns out, our guy G
theorizes is encrypted among
Yea, the waters, Dude.   This is no brachi-
opod, no fossil, this Gilgamesh, whose
nautical prowess, now more prowl than prow,
eludes all scrutiny as we circle

the convivial cove, mounting stairs to
where atop is the moving sidewalk
expediting all suckers and souls, though
not all are tyros who would enter here—
the sharks chauffeured to this revolving door.

Yea, touters among you, the most compe-
tent of Lucifer's legion, cut, run. Make
way, for here wades Leviathan whose heart's
object's no gambol or gamble. Blue chips

the weight of which could cause the earth to pitch
will not detour him from appointed rounds.
*Enkidu. Dude. Wait. There is that we must
now get straight. Eden's tunnel's run's too deep,
too snug to turn back from. Yes, Dude, this means
you. Just as Eve's desire has capaci-
ty to assume a pleasing shape, we are
he as you are me and we are all_____ —hint:
rhyme it with* feather *or* plucked. *Let it fly,
Enkidu; fill in the blank before time
escapes, twenty-three skidoo, from view.* So

this is where thirst drives us—no more stalking;
water awaits our pilgrimage, the mind
enmeshed as if by body stocking. Hence,
none sense this fishy face, largess to dodge
the doorman who, unawares with muffled
yawn, nets not just guests alone but the in-
famous, incognito G, the great catch
of the ages. *Luck's a trade, line of the
unlucky—blind, dumb, then gone. It's a wash,
rebirth. To play the game of some zero.*

Theosophy, this? Or antithesis?
Would it were enough to backfloat the flow,

ease-by the ubiquitous, bloated B's.
No. The hobby we could have gazing at
the lobby's florid ceiling (in spite of
yowls from yon craps tables and bars), a girl-
friend, or two, or three, we could per chance meet,
infatuate, escort, promenade to
virtue or liars' lair—whatever. Or
even skirt it all, traipse counterclockwise

to time and space ante-Cirque du Soleil
when/where Picasso meant energy—not
entropy's eatery, its menu chic,
nauseating, bazaar of the bizarre,
tripe like "Snake Xerophilous sans Cactus."
Yes, Gilgamesh, the serpent's us, Narcis-
sus under glass, coiled, gluttonous gut of
incubus, icon of decadence, the
xenophile possessed by the zodiac.

Enter we now the inner sanctum, Sir
Penance's own vault and penthouse, the most
improbable of grottos, where our shrine
languidly swallows its tail in the form
of tall, perpetual, chocolate falls.
Gone black are the B's bay windows that look
upon tomorrow, pools where we shall lean,
eye the nothing that is our reflection.

III. Z Ain't Just for Zabecedarium

❖ *The Unknown*

Z—symbol as simple as one two three,
yet what a feat, in fact, that, as if an
X-acto knife, a pen in hand divines
what ken can't count on, that tilted tally,
verticals vamped, a ménage-a-tois of
unstaid ink unlike Roman numeral
III or—depending on where the eyes might
sit, in or without a death house cell—mere
rear window to the anteroom of hell,
Q.E.D. one eleven in heaven;
paradise in plain words is a crap shoot,
omega in the alpha, ruse and loose
noose of Judas, unjust jurisprudence
multiplied by that factor known as grace,
luck for some, as in the case of—holy
kudos—auspiciousness in the infant
Jesus while none for the baby Judas.
Identify with one or the other
house—you're the loser. Gospel truth is you've
got to choose even though granted no choice,
for not to choose is choice, in fact, itself,
equivocal as wingspread on a cross.
Default it's called. One less integer or
cog in the hokum of ones and no ones,
binary it would have you believe, though
anode to cathode, the Zodiac zaps.

❖   *Eden Overgrown*

Zzazzip—mute, unadorned music sprung from
you-know-what-but-not-who, who aren't wont to
exit the deepest pocket of the worn
world for our garb. For where but where they are,
vying for numbers, shall they acquire that
unction, that heaven-sent poison in which
to dip their blowgun's dart not for sport but
sustenance, its sound both song and word for
river or rain—any entity or
quantity or quality to which they
point: even rock, even the canopy
onto top of which they climb to say the
name of cloud, which is sky's rock, the same as
mother, as death, which is cause, as well, to
label themselves the Zzazzip—our *pizzazz*
keened backwards over protein even the
Jesuits, urbane angels among them,
identify in their notebooks as "meat."
Hath ye no heathen, Heaven? Half of the
goddamned souls who've salivated on the
face of the earth never heard of saving
eggs (their bacon), let alone salvation.
Donned they no loin cloth, no lord's kain, while we
came able to don earphones, play primal
brethren's breath from, say, though gone, John Lennon—
all that pizzazz shot for naught, that zzazzip.

❖ *The Be and the End-All*

Z ain't just for zabecedarium,
yo mama know, be it a bumblebee's
ecstasy or disappearing ink she
wrote on yo memory, sparklers in the
velvet dark when y'all was but a chile still
unda the spell of her simple magic,
that brand that conjured a bee figin to
see to its deft deed, while in no big-ass
rush to think on its ownself when it's gone
(queen rightly a drone's supreme being), e-
pistemology only fuzzed-up buzz
of what was once adroit ontology.
Now, y'all sees being's alter ego: N
made to lie on its side or, say, the side-
lines where it come to has its lazy ass,
K.O.'d, tackled far shy of the end zone,
jersey ripped all to shit, though you O.K.—
intact, Jack, dude back from bed to mend his
head with vinegar 'n brown paper 'n
good to go, albeit a bit dizzy,
focused on the buzz, that hive alive as
Eden in autumn. Or is you dense, plumb
dumb, sos neva to sense the true human
condition: that hum inside yo helmet,
Boy, ain't hell a'tall till fizzled bulb, Bub,
a noise like sparks snuffed in the starless dark.

❖ *A Part of Speech Apart*

Zounds, oath pronounced "zoondz" lest it sounds as though
yowled through tissue paper and comb, a stiff
xyst of teeth to resist and thus create
with resounding action of the tongue those
vowels gone diphthong though served up round, not
unlike the involuntary "ow" of
torture in the offing or stealth-less pain
suggested by a baby buzz saw that
rips its phoneme from beginning to end.
Quasi-complete, however, is pen light
prosody declining here to compete
openly with an *OED* CD,
never mind words out of context are as
much sounds as they are nouns, verbs, whatever—
linguistic links, except interjections,
kinks in the lines of communication
Joyce himself cannot consecrate what with
infidels of innovation about,
haughty types who somehow believe in a
grammatical relationship between
felicity's fiddle and fixing to
efface the idol of formalism,
duh. The four whores of the apocalypse—
chastity, cheer, charm, camouflage—cannot
be saddled with quartering Christ—just dumb
asses who ride them, braying, "Zounds," (God)'s wounds.

❖   *Pastoral Ethereal*

Z—bold as could be it holds the door's boards
yeoman-like upon the barn's black yawn, no
X on chest to suggest a target, no
weapon shouldered or soldiers wept over,
vectors drawn by moat for lamb, kid, and ass
ugly as cute, air muted, soft, shot with
thecrythecrythecryofthepeacock.
Such is the timbre not of nightmare, raw
renzai having gone awry, but daydreams
quid pro quo. And how is that barnyard bought,
pray tell, without time to do the world right—
ocean to ocean, land and sky—become
naught if not a blind oologist whose
meditation on the feel, the shape, the
locus of points might lead to insight, like
kef, the mind in sync with the *Ur*-egg, Earth.
Jejune as inertia may seem to be,
incubation spawns incunabula,
habit the greater half of habitat,
gravity good practice for the grave, and
focus the floating mote seized lest we see
effing zero, fuzz then followed by . . . o . . . —
dumb from deafness to time's rime—*rhythm*, sure
cure for itch to scratch all dormant thought that
beckons back to barn, where red and within
are mere emblems, more mirrors of the end.

American Bovary (The Cosmetician)

Zip code sans abode: for one, one won one
yet lost all heart in Cleveland, where Madam
X, one's spouse, made it big to then make off
with a dollhouse manufacturer from
Versailles. "Forsooth," her lover crooned to her,
"you learn how false true love when you face the
truth," truth being the manufacturer
sooner than later would fracture his skull,
ramming headboard to topple wall, crying,
"Qui vive!" over his living doll, her rouge
powdered-plump cheeks, those coarse, horsehair lashes
open suddenly, as up she rose, too
nonchalant just for lust, but wantonness
more blind than a pair of glass eyes combined.
Looking down, she loathes her frog prince's drool,
kit, and caboodle; knows she ought haul tail,
jiggle and cleavage, to Cleveland; recant
in grand style to an emasculated
husband; then don her own wand for love of
green bred of her black magic, instead of
funds bled pure white, the spit and miss of spite.
Economics masked in histrionics,
dogged with life in a mirror, poodle turns
cat staring back as if groomed to scratch the
bitch, her itch gone south, home, to her own kind
a la KY, where, for one, one ate one.

Love in the Time of Quantum Mechanics

Zircon cons, but not even a pendant
yea long cons like a diamond—Saks or Brand
X—carbon hardly being forever.
Water, more genuinely speaking, *is*—
vaporized ice. Hold a glass to the light.
You shall possess insight, shall partake of
the spirit world of diamonds, two rungs of
separation from the nether world of
raucousness that is the nesting grounds of
quarks, of squarks, of leptons, of sleptons, of
photons. Photinos? Photons you've seen. Say
"Hola" a Los Photinos, new to the
neighborhood. It's no surprise that with a
million million million atoms known to
live in a teaspoon of water there are
Kilkenny cats, that quarks are quirky, that
just as there are sleepers there are leapers.
It's the whang on Yang that makes for the squarks.
Here he lies in the oral embrace of
good time Yin, the marriage's darker half,
for which its design is homologous,
each of two embryonic states of grace,
deaf to our deft imaginings: Is this
cosmology or numerology?
Be it two, three, four dimensions or ten
a cosmos of sparticles is no gem.

American Masque

"Zodiacal light," I write, blot from thought
"y" in *Why*. Why, slowly surfaces par
excellence a picture of sound of it:
Wh—faint though sonorous trace of Luke and
Vader, florescent hum from their sabers
under a neon horizon. Listen,
the year is 1977.
Star Wars has just been released, is all the
rage. Take radio waves like W-
QRS of riot-roped Detroit: to
pump pomp among soul and pop (classical
or romantic) seems just the ticket for
negrophobes who've flooded the suburbs, as
much as for the brothas, who stays back to
learn—canna Colt 45 in dis hand,
Kool in the otha—how you earns respek,
Jack, some serious dignity, Blood: dude
in the voice of a bad ass James Earl Jones.
Hoist a toast to you unholiest of
ghosts and whatchu gotschu's an Oreo
for an aria—stale one at dat, dat
ever chile (man and girl) unnastands ya'll
doff dat Nazi hat and mask—shore nuf dat
cat ain't but a double dosa ugly,
Bigga's cat, ghastly white black rat cat. Juz
ax Mrs. Dalton's cataracts, Bo. *Shit!*

❖ Making History

Zero gravity or depravity,
yogi or yokel, Roman numeral
X or I, you think you've got a shot and
what you've got is exactly that—one shot.
Victory? Nowadays it's victors' vice,
underwritten by Nike, and we're not
talking goddess but stylized "V," that
"swoosh" so ubiquitous as not to be
read as logo, symbol, or word but a
quip on equipment that doesn't bear it—
phantom confetti. What we need is an
old-fashioned future where what is won is
now to be earned. "You wanna fat loan? Give
me a lien," Nature says, witch that she is.
Likewise, if you want a forest, plant trees.
Keen on poetry? Read. One whose action
jives right with carpe diem sees the day
in his sleep, before which the sheep he counts
have profiles less of lambs, more like mountain
goats, and a proper number of iambs
for that climb to a dream of the sublime.
Every good boy does fine, scales his way back
down inclines where history's his story,
crescendo or no. Absent plot it could
be you: airy obit writ by Mort at
Acme Mortuary, who came up short.

❖ The Rookery

"Zero-zero," says the tower to the
yo-yos, their flight plans in hand, those junior
execs who, through windows of palm pilots,
weather the lousy weather in want of
visibility. Similar's the tale
untold of those flown-to-never-return
tiers of grounded angels in which entire
squadrons took refuge, that sanctuary
rank with a darkness so plumb one cannot,
qua imagination, let alone thought,
perceive to what grave degree is less than
obvious: no unbound limb, no free hand,
no crowbar to pry open a hymnal,
much less concordances to Bibles as
likely squeezed unreadable with all knees
kowtowing to appease the word within.
Justice? It turns out she's one of them, an
interloper who, feigning to right her
halo, undoes the knot of her blindfold,
goes gray as a ghost at a vision of
fowl most foul she cannot tell from feathers
everywhere—condors', vultures', ravens', crows'—
decomposed, no hint, even, or glint of
coal, no diamond shaft, no gravity, this
black hole where the soul goes, sold on itself,
as if, in the first place, there was mercy.

❖   **Acme Academy of the University**
      of Megalomania at Melancholy

Zeno, stoic before there were Stoics,
your colonnade calls, whereupon I scrawl
Xs and Os in the dust as if hugs
were smug gestures at odds with kisses, where
verily you spake unto me, "Howbout
you play yourself a little tic-tac-toe,
the aim to outwait fate?" Or am I all
screwed up, confusing you with that other
rogue from antiquity by the same name,
quorum in this phantom forum of bum
philosophers: novice less paper, the
old boy in back honing scissors, and you,
neo-Zeno, the rock. Moreover, I
must bring to pass the task without ink, must
lilt like doves, while one's double, the soul, is
keelhauled through heck on the senses and back,
jolted dead awake to your namesake's odd
intent upon a rapt paradox of
halving one from illusions of many,
God having flunked Intro to Anthro, the
first twist in this, His less-than-orthodox
enlightenment foisted upon us, His
dark little tryst away from home when it's
common sense He ought to return where He
belongs—no harum-scarum harem of
angels to pluck, "He loves me . . . loves me not."

❖ *Urban Dénouement*

Zombie on the left. Zombie on the right.
You know you're no scarecrow, let alone Christ.
X, nevertheless, marks the spot, the cross-
walk where you stand on the median, that
vicissitudinary attitude
undomesticated creatures are known
to show, perhaps a tooth bearing snarl, when
shit of the pigeon targets the skull and
runs down the nape of the animal's neck,
quietus, as if flesh chose not to crawl,
poised, posing as if for a photo of
one impervious to it all, although
needlessly so, already part of the
mural on the tall glass wall across that
looms in this necropolis such that a
Karloff—Boris, that is—spine erect and
jolly well asleep, bores us, you and me,
I see, with me being the third here who
halts and, like Frankenstein's monster there, stands
glued to shoes tucked in his lead galoshes
for now and beyond perpetuity,
erstwhile the light turned green, turning us dumb,
dullards in a stinging rain of hail hell
casts up like cinders at our shins for sins
born of omission—player and no part,
auteur and no art, hero and no heart.

❖ *Divine Comedies*

Zany's the name on a tongue gone amuck —
"Yeti," as if a sixth brother Marx barks,
expels its syllables in sixty-fourths
which, stuttered, turns the air rubber, Mel Blanc's
voice's inimitable ode haunting
us as when into the crevasse *Goofy*
trips and up from the abyss rises that
slick, primordial yodel of pure fright
reserved for flight with streaming ears for wings.
"Quit," begs the tickle-ees of tickle-er,
pneumatology and aeronautics
of angels aside, while in all truth it's
not less feathers here sought but desire for
more. Are not among the masters of the
last century those who scat its effects —
kaleidosconic their Calliopes?
Jazz in the form of joules, shards of stained glass
in the ears of cubists do not suppress
honed, hopeless groans of the dubbed, that stupid
Godforsaken look and plea, the Elmer
Fudds, the Daffy Ducks, Bullwinkles, Goofys —
every sorry citizen whoever,
duped, would think himself free, now "twapped by a
cwazy contaminated wabbit" that
breathes hilarity with hell's own bellows.
Abominable? Just jokes. That's all. Folks.

❖ ***Another Country***

Zingers you fling like horseshoe ringers. You're
Yorick, faux bonhomme gone deadpan as a
xenolith from the depths of the Devil's
wrack and ruin, or would that be Neptune's?
Vox a la Jack-in-the-box or sirens'
uncharted rocks, your lure's in taboo yore,
tall lore of Earth, where just as down there's fear
so waits faith in nothing to fear up here.
Rebel strain, you point to unmerciful
(Qui s'excuse s'accuse) indelible wind
pummeling hollow grottos below, whole
oceans of undercurrents to propel
nil if not armadas of clouds set sail,
medicine for what ails angels or, at
least, a diversion from the crippling,
kill-joy effects of perfection—torpor's
jaunt, for which there's momentary respite
in this port of call, where all but the saints
have disembarked while the captain takes on
gray cargo here in Limbo, where lobsta
for suppa at the Pockside, Bha Habah
even, let alone pick-up picnics like
dole for gaunt gulls, cannot now detour El
Capitan from his appointed rounds when
bound for bounty in more souls. You? What fool
acts the opossum in clutches of a ghoul?

❖ *Professor Lucifer in the Arena of Angels*

"... zooplasty on a grand scale, Uncle's
yen to adorn the soul with sense beyond
Xs sewn for eyes on sock dolls (Jacko's
watch, no parallax in that lax, cross-eyed
vision: sight sans insight, its dazzled look
under scrutiny), hence, mind, rather, how
the mind, being an appendage to the
soul, is in the scheme of things meat met with
raison d'être for a treat, then the barbe-
cue where for dessert there shall be apple
pie flown back from Eden, a rare entrée
of undetermined fare preceded by
none other than a gangrene salad, a
much-maligned primordial soup, and, at
last, appetizers beneath a spell of
knelling, metaphysical handbells—no
jumbo tolls, no subliminal signal
invoking a horde of winged dogs to the
hunt. O, my incalculable lovelies,
gods of the loft that in such myriad
forms are but air, stacked vapor, and old light
everywhere but where you are, which of you—
deaf ears, hollow eyes, numb tongues, and no thumbs—
can tell me whereabouts besides the foul
bowels I shall make the incision, what
angle take to free from flesh the angel?"

❖   *Zucchini Surprise*

Zucchini Surprise, that original
yummy remembered much more for its size,
ex post facto takes the cakes, lights the lights,
wins ribbons, is gobbled now as the prize.
Voluminous, hence, are the almanacs.
Ubiquitous, therefore, is the seed, for
this is the future, time of hunger and
starvation to make potato famines
resemble hell's hiatus or the Queen's
quay. Cockroaches, entomologists say,
part and parcel, shall inherit the earth.
O so why should one not assume there'll come
no dearth of dirt, when the cockroach also
must eat, asks the last eugenicist, who
loves a twist, dreams of zucchini like a
king cobra to hiss and spit, scare the be
Jesus out of it—the cockroach, that is—
instead of—before the bombs—a mongoose.
Had hell no hunger would it still be hell?
Go figure: to take away one leaves none.
For the final feast there shall be, at most,
each an eater and eaten, then, at least,
defecation, if not defecator.
Child of Kafka, imagine: in an old
bed of manure the cockroach awoke
and found himself to be a zucchini.

❖   *Tabloid Behemoth*

ZOOMORPH SPIED, TAGGED GOD'S LYCANTHROPY
Yellow journalism? Steaming urine:
xanthic, yes, that fog that rubs its back on
window-panes, feline sometimes, sometimes sphinx,
vagrant from on-high where Vs of geese might
undulate across the face of the moon
to flash sporadic hints of a burned out
sign of the divine, where shapeshifters out
run a golden sun, an Olivier
quizzing a blind Polonius: HAM. to
POL.: ". . . see yonder cloud that's almost in shape
of a camel?" POL.: "By the mass, and 'tis
[no aside] like a camel indeed." HAM.:
"Methinks it is like a weasel." POL.: ". . . backed
like a weasel." HAM.: "Or like a whale?" POL.:
[kin in candlelight] "Very like a whale."
Jaundice? Yuk, yuk, the yolk's not on us but
inextricable, we butter beware,
had not without us when pol means people,
good citizens like sunflowers slowly
following with their eyes the parent sun.
Evening, now. All heads drooping, these standing
dreamers in afterglow, its bane in the
calm, colossal creeping of earth's shadow
before their being overcome by sleep,
aware not whether will come dawn or death.

❖ The Watchers and the Watched

Zeitgeists like this mean more museum heists,
yule logs the size of toothpicks, and a Rol-
ex on all our lists instead of Timex,
which, as Christmas wishes go, is not as
vain, not opulent, oddly, as it sounds
utilitarian, the greatest good
the grandest goods for the greatest number.
Somehow somewhere sometime something almost
rococo burrowed in the soul not to
quaff from an empty vessel but, like a
psychological corkscrew, take hold, pop
open the bottle to release from its
nascent state the desire to be fulfilled.
Meanwhile, there are culture's accoutrements,
like rescued tapestries of the past or
K-rations in the form of film cans for
Johns and Janes Doe, who, in contrast to an
infinite number of names for numbers,
have not known nor sought the dignity that
goes ink in pen with an identity.
Face it, with film as the mirror of our
era, only the faceless can save face,
drawn to both sides of the proscenium,
characters like actors actors portray
benighted with pseudonyms for a blind
audience that cannot tell them from them.

❖   *Arse Poetica*

Zigzagging invisibly like noiseless
yelps, these indelible paths of rabbits
exiting their nest when in fact the nest
was no hole in which you tripped but collapsed
velvet top hat that in the next instant
upon your head in your dream seems as if
the proper accent, as otherwise you
stand irrevocably naked in a
rain of intermittent applause stopped off
cue, clue you are not—never have been—the
prestidigitator billed to be here
on fire but flaming asshole whose issue
notwithstanding your audience is you,
more flatulence to rhyme with raspberries,
less scatological than kazoo-like
kudos from those whose deafening dose of
juvenility you deliver does
indeed deserve wan delight yet instructs
hoards of the hearing-impaired how now to
grin in the face of the grimace reaper,
focusing upon your pert, prosthesis
ears, your bulbous proboscis for nose, your
diminutive and dimly lit eyes cir-
cumscribed by the black licorice rims and
bows, phony glasses summarily tucked
and slipped up the sleeve of your nakedness.

Ode Over a Coffee Table Book

Zoophiles all—thumbing here thither and
yon—the we in me, schizoid devotee
ex parte of one Tooker, George, painter
with an ear as well as eye for what the
vulnerable don't say yet say in their
unlocked cages (their cubicles, their stalls,
the walls), a haze like mirror mist on some
scenes, doors off their hinges for others—or
are we (prism light imprisoned by these
quadrangles of ink that lure us to tight
proximity while the periphery,
once laser sharp, now goes soft), are we then
no better off that we empathize thus,
myopic, anima among us the
listlessness of animus, given what
kain from anima animus feeds each
jour maigre on, minus will, stamina, plus
ill aim? We ought to free these creatures, these
humans, close the book like a tourniquet's
grip on their silence, which is the bleeding,
forever bleating herd—the *real* subject
everywhere nowhere in all of Tooker,
devoid the Shepherd from whom and for whom
comes no word. Compulsively we thumb on,
become, simply, a monk-like presence in
absence of the complex of our strangeness.

❖ Less Is More

"Zabwino," they say in Chichewa (no
yokemate to English, its alphabet sans
X), translated as "good things will happen,"
which my tutor utters with such faith, such
verve, I flinch with pure pecuniary
umbrage at his steep charity, as he
trades a priceless word for a two bit phrase
so—praise all blessings—I in turn read how
rich would be a world for which the play in
Q & A's without question answer to
problems unplumbed by an alphabet with-
out not only an X—but a Q, too.
Nudged to weigh anew, I sense twenty-six
minus X & Q's more than twenty-four,
leave door ajar on the lid of this I-
kid-ye-not, fixed, ready-mix metaphor
jamb-packed where the abstract meets the concrete.
Eye to eye, I ask Alistarico
how then in Chichewa one says *question*
(green again, the tongue tastes fun), so he goes,
"Funso." "Say *what*?" I say. He says, "Funso."
Ever so slowly the o on his lips
deflates as though through a closing hatch I
see a ladder he now retracts, heading
back, while I'm left to man the moon—wise guy
all agog—cross my heart and trope to vie.

❖ A Routine Physical

"Zomax," she reads aloud, the student nurse,
"You're still allergic to it?" *That's one R-
x they axed*, I nearly blurt back, tongue still
wringing itself dry of wrath, bathed in the
vile, mild bile of impatience. Of course I
understand that she asks. One must play-act
to earn license to practice, just as I've
sat, cool and fuming, relearning how to
relax, waiting my turn, chalked against mis-
cue of memory. "It killed a bunch of
people," I softly say. "Oh?" she goes, bent
on my chart, busy with her own business.
"Noxious stuff, Zomax. They took it off the
market before you were born." Now her head
lifts, her eyelids with it. "Ah," she says with
ken, yet the curiosity of Doc's
jar of Popsicle sticks, so that just then
is the moment—as she raises her watch,
having reached for my pulse—for which I so
gently take in my right hand her left wrist
for reasons I don't understand until
even she seems to see it: how close rose
death's old ghost on the drive here, heat ahead
coming off the pavement, invisible
bees swarming in hives of air and white light.
"Eh . . . ," I say, "no rush. The good Doc will wait."

❖   ## Snapshots

Zzazzip. Old Gladhappy here. Another
year. A window on the Thanatopsis
Express and you the engineer with a
whistle, a party favor, its zzazzip.
"Vamoos," you spit at the photographer
until photographer gets the picture:
the cowcatcher's on the caboose, the train's
stopped, this shot of you with the look of a
Ray Carver under the weather, on the
q.t. about where you're coming from (the
pane of a phone booth?). What's there but to dial
O, though slow to do so, to disclose woe
no noble plotter ought to opt to pose;
moreover, was it not John Gardner who
laments, *Sure death for the poet is to
keep the wound closed*? Chivas in one hand, Georg
Jensen briar in the other, there you are
incarnate, austere, Sir Carver Gardner.
Holy steak and cake! Holy omnivore!
Great green gobs of greasy, grimy gopher!
For what? For the gusto? Or for "it," what-
ever it is sits in the gut so low,
drives you to chug and smoke, and causes the
camera to capture by missing it—point
being the point of being's not to quit,
addict of the rush in hissing, "Screw it."

Loss

Zonked with thought of a long life lived honked off,
you adopt a new m.o. Each box you
x, no or yes, on the mind's check list, this
walking cyclopedia of friends' deaths,
vindicates, as you bear witness to grace
under the dome of autumn—and the lack
thereof. Grief, you guess, is like this, like a
spider's fidgeting digits you did not
recognize as the heart before you caught
quivering needles of light between fence
posts as far apart as a pair of arms
out flung, though strung so thin to have become
next to nothing, on legs, but a two di-
mensional rib cage. O web of sorrows
like the ghost of a skeleton, like the
keeper of holes. O geometry of
jackstraws, emaciated scarecrow, Christ
in the corn, guard of the garden till dark,
here going, going, though for now not quite
gone. O impalpable loss, the heart lost,
found slave to itself bound in illusion,
emptiness swelling with the broad moon's face
dawning, donning its mask, revealing its
crypt's secret: autumn's neither sun nor leaf
but mirage gleaned by the insidious
angst in us, light of the mirror's montage.

❖ Shining

Zapped in the back with a Rayovac beam's
yards of teeming mist, this live planetoid
X (that might as well be light years from us)
wedged in a fork of paper birch (inert
victim of blind, benign voyeurism,
unfazed by the likes of us lowlifes) lies
the cub porcupine, whose guise at dusk, a
scrub brush turned up (sans any chance in a
race from us, tortoise, or tamest of lame
quadrupeds), but with a gorgeous hue of
pewter so rare as to be the sheer form
of itself that (in urgent fervor to
name in order to more perfectly re-
member) a Plato might call angelware—
light the gown angels wear, their gossamer
karma aura's alloy in the ideal—
jerry built, as is always the human
idea of the beautiful, when our
history has yet to happen on some
godforsaken, lopsided moon on the
far edge of the farthest galaxy, where
eons from now sparsest particles rain
down in a mist of emptiness here sensed,
coveting the porcupine's seeming o-
bliviousness to angst and bliss alike,
as hid in its caterpillar crawl—wings.

for Joanne Lowery

❖ *A Disappearing Act*

Zowie, word in a hummingbird heard—gone.
"Yikes!"—what it seems to say with its lofty
exit, its scaredy cat, peek-a-boo play.
We the peephole to hell, perhaps, remain
virginal in terms of maiden flight to
unparalleled heights, but on unchaste chase
to unearth heaven here, I say, "Holy
scat, no angel if not Tinkerbell's soul
rates wings like those." Still, should time come for res-
cue—fire or ice—would I kowtow? Does the
pope in his garden clamor for ladder
overhead, that bee-line and blur in the
noise of the hummingbird, thin rope of hope
more like from a toy helicopter and
less a flying saucer? I don't *think* so.
Kaput means kibosh, ash for balderdash,
je ne sais pas. Dares one stare dead in the
eye of the beholder seeking beauty
here with a mirror, or does one shudder,
gnostic who pictures black behind the glass?
For fortitude—out of fortune, fear or
egress—is faint ally to existence,
dawn the round nemesis of time's eclipse,
cyclical as it is, as is the coy
buzz, the quick charge, the discrete retreat of
all muse, that, game won, song sung, vanishes.

Printed in the United States
200588BV00002B/67-186/A